REMEMBERING

WILLIAM CARLOS WILLIAMS

D1563475

WILLIAM CARLOS WILLIAMS

REMEMBERING

WILLIAM CARLOS WILLIAMS

James Laughlin

A NEW DIRECTIONS BOOK

A Note on Metric

In composing this book I intentionally avoided rhetoric and verbal decoration. A tone of colloquial speech and a fast pace for reading were intended. To describe the metric I would use the term narrative verse. It is not lyric poetry. It is descriptive rather than critical in commenting on Williams's work. A friend has called it a "good receptacle for recollections."

The meter is based on the free-verse, essentially three-beat line which my old friend and mentor Kenneth Rexroth perfected in his travel poem *The Dragon & the Unicorn*, which I published at New Directions in 1952. Rexroth admired Williams and his work. I have appended his moving tribute to Williams at the end of the book.

This text is a segment from James Laughlin's long poem-in-progress, *Byways*. While nothing of substance has been changed, certain quotations from William Carlos Williams' letters and prose writings have been compressed for space and/or altered for clarity of reference. For acknowledgments and photo credits, please see p.64.

Manufactured in the United States of America
Designed by Leslie Miller, The Grenfell Press
New Directions Books are printed on acid-free paper.
First published as New Directions Paperbook 811 in 1995
Published simultaneously in Canada by Penguin Books Canada Limited

Library of Congress Cataloging-in-Publication Data

Laughlin, James, 1914–
    Remembering William Carlos Williams / James Laughlin.
        p.   cm.
    ISBN 0-8112-1307-2 (pbk.)
    1. Williams, William Carlos, 1883-1963—Poetry. 2. Poets, American—20th century—Poetry. 3. Poetics—Poetry.   I. Title.
PS3523.A8245R46   1995
811'.52—dc20
                                                            59-15719
                                                            CIP

New Directions Books are published for James Laughlin
by New Directions Publishing Corporation,
80 Eighth Avenue, New York 10011

9 RIDGE ROAD

A not large, unpretentious
Wooden house, the clapboards
Painted a dull mustard color,
Two stories and an attic, set
On a little slope over the
Street level, with steps and
An iron railing going up;
By the door was a small sign:
9 Ridge Road. W.C. Williams,
MD. Please ring bell. The house
Must have been built at about
The time of World War One
And stands on an avenue of
Maple trees where the little
Business center of Rutherford
(NJ) merges into an area of
Comfortable homes inhabited
By commuters to New York,
Middle-class people mostly.
No super-highways in those
Days; by bus it was a boring
Hour's journey across the
Wetlands to Manhattan.

To this shrine, a supplicant,
I came a year after Pound had
Coaxed me into trying to become
A publisher, promising to write
His friends who might have books
That needed doing. William Carlos
Williams—What a magical name!—
Was one to whom he had written.
I was a-tremble to barge in on
One of my literary idols, who
Was not yet famous with the general
Public, but in the underground
Of the literary avant-garde,
Such as we'd heard about in
Boarding school, along with
Pound, he was supreme. *Kora in*

KORA IN HELL
IMPROVISATIONS

By WILLIAM CARLOS WILLIAMS

Hell and *Spring and All* had
Been sacred texts in Dudley
Fitts's honors class at Choate.
I was afraid that Williams when
He saw how young I was would
Send me packing. What would he
Be like? I climbed the steps and
Rang the bell. A woman opened.
This would be Floss, his wife,
Telling me the doctor was with
A patient, to take a seat in the
Parlor, I was expected. A very
Ordinary room, somewhat shabby
Furniture. But the paintings
On the walls: a cubist Demuth
Of industrial smokestacks and
Two slender Demuth flowers; a
Precisionist Sheeler bowl of
Fruit; a Dove and a Marin; a
Colorful Ben Shahn abstraction
Of a building that seemed to be
All eyes. These were gifts from
His painter friends. Also a
Marsden Hartley, pale mountains
In New Mexico. Later on Bill
Told me that Hartley had been
A pest, trying to make passes.

After a wait the doctor came in
With his white coat on, a big
Smile, very welcoming. Without
Reserve he told me an anecdote
About the patient he had just
Been treating. All doors were
Open. Bill was a non-cutaneous
Man. No skin separated him from
Others. A new acquaintance was
At once a friend. He had no
Side. His speech was broken now
And then by an extraordinary goat
Laugh. Floss joined us, a small
Sturdy woman, serious, laconic.

She did not smile too easily.
She suffered from a buzzing in
One ear, the result of a whip-
Lash when Bill was driving the
Car and had to put on the brakes
Suddenly. Patient, enduring Floss.
Being married to such a bundle
Of energy as Bill couldn't have
Been easy for her.

Bill and I first talked about
Pound, they had been friends
In college. What was the old
Nut up to now? Then about Bill's
Two sons, Paul and William
Eric, one still in school, one
Starting college. Neither much
Interested in writing, and just
As well too, hardly a career
To recommend to a son, all
That grief he'd had getting his
Early books published. Twenty
Years ahead of what was then
Accepted by most readers. Bill
Had had to pay for publication
Of his first five books: the
Poems of 1909 (sold for 35¢
And not many sold at that, in
Garroway's Stationery store),
*Al Que Quiere, Kora in Hell,
Spring and All* and *The Great
American Novel* (which wasn't
A novel at all). And when he
Finally found a commercial
Publisher to do his *Voyage to
Pagany*, the firm went bankrupt.
So Bill was desperate, he was
Willing to take a chance on
A 22-year-old neophyte. We
Decided that *White Mule*, his
Novel in which Floss is born on
The first page, would be our

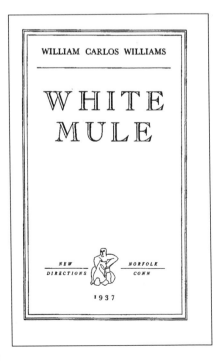

WILLIAM CARLOS WILLIAMS

WHITE
MULE

NEW
DIRECTIONS

NORFOLK
CONN

1937

Beginning, and from there we'd
Go on to its sequels in the Stecher
Trilogy, which tells the history
Of Floss's German immigrant
Family. Before I left 9 Ridge
Road Floss and Bill took me to
See their flower garden, a small
Plot behind the kitchen stoop.
This was Bill's favorite hobby.
Over a hundred poems on
Flowers and trees may be found
In his books. A florilegium.

On October 27, 1936, what a
Momentous day for me and for
New Directions, I found at
The post office a letter that
Was addressed to the deity.
"Dear God," it began, "You
Mention, casually, that you
Are willing to publish my
White Mule, that you will pay
For it and that we shall then
Share, if any, the profits!
My God! It must be that you
Are so tall that separate
Clouds circle around that head,
Giving thoughts of other metal
Than those the under sides of
Which we are in the habit of
Seeing." *White Mule* was a
Success; Bill's first and my
First. Good critics reviewed
It. The book was talked about.
We did a second printing. I
Could walk into a shop with my
Wares and not be regarded as a
Crazy young freak. Bill's fame
Rubbed off on his old friend
Pound, whose books soon began
To move a bit as they had not
Before. A door opened. A new

To Be

(Floss's birth, the opening lines
of White Mule)

She entered, as Venus from the
sea, dripping. The air enclosed
her, she felt it all over her,
touching, waking her. If Venus
did not cry aloud after release
from the pressures of that sea-
womb, feeling the new and
lighter flood springing in her
chest, flinging out her arms—
this one did. Screwing up her
tiny smeared face, she let out
three convulsive yells—and lay
still.

The Locust Tree in Flower

Among
the leaves
bright

green
of wrist-thick
tree

an old
stiff broken
branch

ferncool
swaying
loosely strung—

come May
again
white blossom

clusters
hide
to spill

their sweets
almost
unnoticed

down
and quickly
fall

9

From *Perpetuum Mobile: The City*

      —a dream
we dreamed
      each
separately
      we two

of love
      and of
desire—

that fused
in the night—

in the distance
      over
the meadows
      by day
impossible—
      The city
disappeared
      when
we arrived—

      A dream
a little false

toward which
      now
we stand
      and stare
transfixed—

All at once
      in the east
rising!

      All white!
      small
as a flower—

a locust cluster

Period in American literature
Began. We went to press with
Bill's stories, *Life Along the
Passaic River*, and not long after
With a *Collected Poems*.

On a later visit to 9 Ridge Road
Bill walked me up the hill back
Of his house. From the top there
Was a wide and open view across
The wetlands to the skyscrapers
Of Manhattan which rose like
White flowers through the haze.
In his early years New York City
Was a tantalizing enigma, "a
Dream of love and of desire,"
He called it in one poem, "a
Dream a little false." It was a
Menacing illusion. When he was
Interning at French Hospital
On 10th Avenue, then at Child's
Hospital uptown, Bill thought
About a lucrative practice in
The city. Manhattan was where
Writers and artists lived; he
Made many friends among them
In Greenwich Village. But he
Found other things he didn't
Care for. Ceaseless movement.
Corruption. Greed. Violence.
Tensions. The sense grew in him
That the area where he had grown
Up—Rutherford and the other
New Jersey towns around Paterson—
Was his *locus mirabilis*, where
He belonged and would be happiest,
The place where he was destined
To do his doctoring and also
Try to capture in his poetry
The sounds of the local speech
And the small-town folkways.
How did Bill manage to be a

10

Full-time pediatrician as well
As an obstetrician: hospital
Hours, office hours? House
Calls, night calls? And then
To write some thirty books on
Top of that. Drafting poems
On prescription slips as he
Drove in his car, writing
Stories on yellow pads as he
Waited for a woman to give
Birth, going up to his desk
In the attic to type for an
Hour or so after a night call.
Of course he had great strength
And vitality. But in the end
He paid for the drain on his
Body; he paid with the strokes
That crippled him in old age.
The secret was, I'm sure, that
His careers were complementary;
They fed on each other; together
They nourished him. He himself
Explains it thus in the chapter
"Of Medicine and Poetry" in his
Autobiography: "They ask me how
I have continued an equal interest
In medicine and the poem, I reply
That they amount for me to nearly
The same thing. The cured man
Is no different from any other.
It is a trivial business unless
You add the zest to the picture.
That's how I came to
Find writing such a necessity.
My "medicine" was the thing which
Gained me entrance to these secret
Gardens of the self. I was
Permitted by my medical badge
To follow the poor, defeated
Body into those gulfs and grottos.
Just there, the thing, in all
Its greatest beauty, may for

...
a dream
           toward which
we love—
at night
                 more
than a little
             false—

Complaint

They call me and I go.
It is a frozen road
past midnight, a dust
of snow caught
in the rigid wheeltracks.
The door opens.
I smile, enter and
shake off the cold.
Here is a great woman
on her side in the bed.
She is sick,
perhaps vomiting,
perhaps laboring
to give birth to
a tenth child. Joy! Joy!
Night is a room
darkened for lovers,
through the jalousies
      the sun
has sent one gold needle!
I pick the hair from
      her eyes
and watch her misery
with compassion.

From *Asphodel, That Greeny Flower*

...
      At the altar
            so intent was I
before my vows,
      so moved by your presence
            a girl so pale
and ready to faint
      that I pitied
            and wanted to protect you.
As I think of it now,
      after a lifetime
            it is as if
a sweet-scented flower
      were poised
            and for me did open.

...
an odor
      as from our wedding
            has revived for me
and begun again to penetrate
      into all crevices
            of my world.

From *Many Loves*

Women! With their small
heads and big lustrous
eyes. All my life I have
never been able to escape
them.

A moment be freed to fly
Guiltily about the room.
For a split second it has
Fluttered before me, a
Phrase which I quickly
Write down on anything at
Hand, any piece of paper
I can grab."

In 1912 Bill was married to
Florence Herman, the younger
Of two sisters. She had thought
He would marry her older sister,
Charlotte, but he was turned
Down. In frustration he courted
The younger girl. It is reported
That Bill told Floss that he
Didn't yet really love her but
In time he would. Hardly a very
Romantic proposal. "She must
Take him as he was, a poet, and
Together they'd work it out."
Which is what happened. Many
Years later when in old age
Bill wrote "Asphodel, That
Greeny Flower," the poem that
Was his final declaration of
Love for Floss and his apology
For his infidelities, he had a
Different view of their marriage.
It's common knowledge that
Bill had affairs; not to
The degree of womanizing,
Not satyriasis. He simply
Liked women, drew material
For his work from them. And
Women very much liked him.
After I'd first taken my wife,
Ann, to 9 Ridge Road she told
Me, "That is the most sexy
Man I think I've ever met."
He was kindly and enticing.

Perhaps it came from his mix
Of English and Spanish blood:
English father and Spanish
Mother from Puerto Rico. Bill
Didn't suppress his problem.
He felt guilty about it, he
Hated to hurt Floss, but
Bill's remorse, though it is
Clouded, comes through in his
Play, *A Dream of Love*. It is
A double dream. In the first,
Dr.Thurber, physician and poet,
Takes a neighbor's young wife
To a hotel in New York. Making
Love, he has a heart attack
And dies. In the second dream
He returns to the kitchen of
His home to explain what he
Has done to his grief-stricken
Wife. The explanation is in
Two parts. The first sets out
The role of woman in imagination.
The second, which must have been
Hard for Floss to take, suggests
That an occasional adultery is
Necessary to renew the fervor
Of connubial love.

I

Doc: A man must protect his
integrity as a man, as best he is able,
by whatever invention he can cook
up out of his brains or his belly. He
must create a woman of some sort
out of his imagination to prove him-
self. It's a woman—even if it's a
mathematical formula for relativity.
Even more so in that case—but a
woman. All right, a poem. I mean a
woman, bringing her up to the light,
building her up and not merely of
stone or colors or silly words, but in
the flesh, warm, agreeable, made of
pure consents.

And just as a woman must produce
out of her female belly to complete
herself—a son—so a man must pro-
duce a woman, in full beauty out of
the shell of his imagination and pos-
sess her, to complete himself also...

II

Myra: I don't care what you do
but I demand that you tell me what
you promised this woman before you
dropped dead in bed with her.

...

Doc: Darling, don't let that
bother you. I knew that if we were
to keep on loving each other some-
thing had to be done about it. This
opportunity offered itself and I took
it. To keep love alive....It went all
right. I loved you as a consequence,
more than I ever loved you in my
life up to that time. It worked. I
couldn't tell you—you couldn't have
understood what I felt.

This Is Just to Say

I have eaten
the plums
that were in
the icebox

and which
you were probably
saving
for breakfast

Forgive me
they were delicious
so sweet
and so cold

And Floss's reply

Dear Bill: I've made a
couple of sandwiches for you.
In the icebox you'll find
blueberries—a cup of
              grapefruit
a glass of cold coffee.

On the stove is the teapot
with enough tea leaves
for you to make tea if you
prefer—Just light the gas,
boil the water and put in
              the tea

Plenty of bread in the
              breadbox
and butter and eggs—
I didn't know just what to
make for you. Several people
called up about office hours.

See you later. Love. Floss.

Please switch off the phone.

We get a clearer picture of
Domestic affection at 9 Ridge
Road if we look at what I
Call the "icebox poems." When
Floss or Bill wanted to leave
A message for the other a note
Would be pasted up on the door
Of the kitchen refrigerator:

And there was Cynthia, that
Vivacious girl, who worked
For Capezio's (they made shoes
For ballet dancers) and lived
In Charles Street in the Village,
Announcing with embarrassment
That she was knocked up and
Most likely it was mine. Hardly
A case for my family doctor.
Bill thought it was funny. He
Found an old Italian woman in
Ho-Ho-Kus who took care of the
Matter for $200. Luckily she
Knew her stuff; there were no
Complications. Cynthia settled
Down and married a nice young
Professor at CCNY.

For a man of such manic energy
Bill was even-tempered. He was
Not quarrelsome; he wore a
Mantle of lovable good humor.
In his arguments with his old
Friend Ezra Pound, who was
Forever badgering him about
Something, he was usually very
Indulgent. But there was one
Surprising exception: he hated
T.S. Eliot (whom he never
Met) and went out of his way
To broadcast his antipathy.
What Bill wrote about Eliot
Sounds now like a paranoid

Obsession. Bill saw Eliot as
A traitor who had left his
Country and its culture to go
Over to the British. To sense
The depth of Bill's rage we
Must try to understand how he
Felt, how some other American
Poets felt, when *The Waste Land*
Was published in 1922 with a
Success that carried all before
It. The literary landscape was
Altered overnight, obliterating,
Bill felt, the importance of
His own experimental work.

Since 1913 Bill had been feeling
His way, struggling, toward an
American idiom for poetry, a
Style built from American speech
And the sense of American locality.
The powerful impact of Eliot's
Anglo-francophile verse bowled
Him over. The letter to Pound
At right, which mixes bitterness
With venom, was written
In March of 1939.

With the passage of time, as
Bill's poetic reputation grew,
As the literary and academic
Worlds began to accept his
Concept of an "American idiom"
For poetry, he calmed down
About Eliot. But he had hurt
Himself in England. It took me
Twenty years to find a London
Publisher who would take on
His books, and in the end it
Was a firm set up by Granada
Films that took the risk, not
One of the old-line publishers.
And when Robert Lowell, still

From the *Autobiography*

The Waste Land wiped out our
world as if an atom bomb had been
dropped upon it and our brave sal-
lies into the unknown were turned
to dust.
  To me especially it struck like a
sardonic bullet. I felt at once that it
had set me back twenty years....
Critically Eliot returned us to the
classroom just at the moment when
I felt that we were on the point of
an escape to matters much closer to
the essence of a new art form
itself—rooted in the locality which
should give it fruit...

From a letter from Williams to Pound

I'm glad you like Eliot's verse, but
I'm warning you, the only reason it
doesn't smell is that it's synthetic.
Maybe I'm wrong, but I distrust
that bastard more than any writer I
know in the world today. He can
write, granted, but it's like walking
into a church to me. I can't do it
without a bad feeling at the pit of
my stomach. Nothing has been
learned there since the simplicities
were prevented from becoming mul-
tiform by arrested growth. Bird's-
eye foods, suddenly frozen at fifty
degrees below zero, under pressure,
at perfect maturity, immediately
after being picked from the can.
It's pathological with me perhaps, I
hope not, but I am infuriated by
such things. I am infuriated because
the arrest has taken place, just at the
point of risk, just at the point where
the magnificence might possibly
have happened, just when the dan-
ger threatened, when the tradition
might have led to the difficult new

15

things. But the God damn liars
prefer popes, prefer order, prefer
freezing, prefer if you use the image,
'the sterilization of the Christ they
profess.' And the result is canned to
make literature, with all the flavor,
with all the pomp, while the real
thing rots under their noses and
they duck to the other side of the
street. I despise and detest them.
They are moles on a pig's belly
instead of tits. Christ, how I hate
their guts and the more so because
Eliot, like his monumental wooden
throne on wheels, that he carries
around with him to worship, Eliot
takes the place of the realizable
actual, which is that much held back
from realization precisely, of
existence.

From *I Wanted to Write a Poem*

I had known always that I wanted to
write a long poem but I didn't know
what I wanted to do until I got the
idea of a man identified with a city.
What city? I'd known about
Paterson, even written about it.
Suddenly it dawned on me I had a
find. The Falls [of the Passaic River
near Paterson] were spectacular; the
river was a symbol handed to me.
This was my river and I was going
to use it. I had grown up on its
banks...

Later, tried to bring about
A reconciliation, his efforts
Were not successful.

As the successive volumes of
Pound's *Cantos* were published
By New Directions, with praise
Taking the place of ridicule
And incomprehension, the idea
Grew in Bill's mind that he too
Should be at work on a long poem,
A "personal epic" as the *Cantos*
Were coming to be known. Fair
Enough, the friendly rivalry of
College days would continue.
But what kind of a poem should
It be? Obviously nothing like
The *Cantos*, either in content
Or technique. The *Cantos* were
International, ranging through
Every culture except that of
Latin America. But Bill's poem
Must be as American as the idiom
In which it would be written.
It would be New Jersey American
And its name would be *Paterson*,
The city near which he had been
Born and whose people he knew
So well from his doctoring.
For his symbol Bill took the
Passaic River as it follows its
Course down to the sea. He felt
That his life was like that
Of the river. At first he
Worried about the verse,
Then let the form take
Care of itself, permitting
Colloquial language to set the
Pace, flowing as easily as
The river flowed. He called his
Protagonist "Dr. Paterson," but
When he spoke of Paterson he

Meant both the man and the city.
They were the same. Yet for
The structure of the poem they
Had complementary identities.
Paterson was conceived, but
So much detailing remained
To be worked out. It became
Almost a life work. The first
Notes for the poem in the
Williams archive at Buffalo
Date from 1926. The first
Volume appeared in 1946, the
Second in 1948, the third in
1949, the fourth in 1951, and
The fifth in 1958. Bill often
Used to say, "This is the last
Of *Paterson*, Jim," but it wasn't
And in 1963 after he died we
Found notes for more pages. It
Might have gone on a long time
Further, partly because Bill
Agonized so much about it and was
Churned by such self-doubt. He
Often felt he had not found
The needed cohesive threads
For the work, and that his
Great poem, a whole life of
Writing, thought, and vision,
Was inevitably a failure.
At right is a letter he wrote
To me in December of 1943.

One problem in the publication
Of *Paterson* was to devise a
Distinctive typographical
Format for the text pages of
The book. For his early poems
Bill used a conventional page
Layout: a fixed left margin
Without indentations, regular
Vertical spacings, no half
Lines, few eccentricities in

Author's Note to *Paterson Part I*

This is the first part of a long poem
in four parts—that a man in himself
is a city, beginning, seeking, achiev-
ing and concluding his life in ways
which the various aspects of a city
may embody—if imaginatively con-
ceived—any city, all the details of
which may be made to voice his
most intimate convictions. Part One
introduces the elemental character of
the place. The Second Part will
comprise the modern replicas. Three
will seek a language to make them
vocal, and Four, the river below the
falls, will be reminiscent of
episodes—all that one man may
achieve in a lifetime.

Letter from WCW to JL, 1943

That God damned and I mean God
damned poem *Paterson* has me
down. I am burned up to do it but
don't quite know how. I write and
destroy, write and destroy. It's all
shaped up in outline and intent, the
body of the thinking is finished but
the technique, the manner and the
method are unresolvable to date. I
flounder and flunk.

And another in November, 1948

I get moments of despair over
Paterson, the usual thing, a feeling
that I'm through for life, just a
wash-out. Something lower than the
lowest. Then again I spark along for
a few lines and think I'm a genius.
The usual crap. I'll do the best I
can.

on a log, her varnished hair
trussed up like a termite's nest (forming
the lines) and, her old thighs
gripping the log reverently, that,
all of a piece, holds up the others—
alert: begin to know the mottled branch
that sings   .

certainly NOT the university,
a green bud fallen upon the pavement its
sweet breath suppressed: Divorce (the
language stutters)

unfledged:

two sisters from whose open mouths
Easter is born—crying aloud,

Divorce!

While
the green bush sways: is whence
I draw my breath, swaying, all of a piece,
separate, livens briefly, for the moment
unafraid   .   .

Which is to say, though it be poorly
said, there is a first wife
and a first beauty, complex, ovate—
the woody sepals standing back under
the stress to hold it there, innate

Deployment. It was tame-cat
Layout, nothing modern
About it. For *Paterson* he
Wanted something far more
Visual and expressive. Broken
Lines, short lines mixed with
Long lines, variations in
Vertical spacing, in short
A page where the type would
Float free, as unrestrained as
The ideas the words were stating.
He wanted to liberate the words
And lines on the page. Bill had
A strong visual sense. As a young
Man he had done some creditable
Painting. From the days of the
Armory Show of 1913 he had been
Interested in painting and had
Close painter friends. From his
Trips to Europe he knew what
Apollinaire had done with his
Calligrammes and how the Dadaists
And Surrealists had experimented
With typography. It was only
Natural that he should conceive
Of a page of type as a free-form
Design. When I showed Bill's
Script to our salesman at Haddon
Craftsmen, the commercial printer
New Directions often used, he
Said that such composition
Would cost an arm and a leg;
The irregular spacing couldn't
Be done by linotype. By luck I
Had heard of a small printer,
George W. Van Vechten in
Metuchen, New Jersey, who
Enjoyed solving typographical
Problems in books. Bill and
Van Vechten took to each other.
The compositor sensed at once
The forms that the poet was

See the sample page from *Paterson I.*
Note the emphasis obtained by the
extra vertical spacing around
'unfledged' and 'Divorce!' Note how
the wide spacing of the dots after the
first and fourth paragraphs extends
the breath pauses. The heavily
indented three words would not have
been found in poems of a decade
earlier. The omission of page
numbers causes the type blocks to
float on the page as if this were a
drawing. Is there a bit of literary
history in this layout, the prototype
of the kind of free verse we practice
now as a matter of course, and of the
structure which Denise Levertov
calls 'organic form'?

PATERSON
(B O O K   O N E)

A NEW
DIREC-
TIONS
BOOK

WILLIAM CARLOS
WILLIAMS

From WCW to Parker Tyler, 1948

All the prose, including the tail
which would have liked to have
wagged the dog, has primarily the
purpose of giving a metrical meaning
to or of emphasizing a metrical con-
tinuity between all word use. It is
not an antipoetic device, the repeat-
ing of which piece of miscalculation
makes me want to puke. It *is* that
prose and verse are both *writing*,
both a matter of the words and an
interrelation between words for the
purpose of exposition, or other bet-
ter defined purpose of *the art.* Please
do not stress other 'meanings.' I
want to say that prose and verse are
to me the same thing, that verse (as
in Chaucer's tales) belongs *with*
prose, as the poet belongs with
'Mine Host,' who says in so many
words to Chaucer, 'Namoor, all that
rhyming is not worth a toord.'
Poetry does not *have* to be kept
away from prose as Mr. Eliot might
insist, it goes *along with* prose and,
companionably, by itself, without aid
or excuse or need for separation or
bolstering, shows itself by *itself* for
what it is. *It belongs* there, in the
gutter. Not anywhere else or wher-
ever it is, it is the same: the poem.

Groping for, and gave him many
Proofs set in various ways to
Choose from. I wish I'd urged
Bill to dedicate *Paterson* to
George. This was a case where
An intuitive designer helped
Perfect a great work.

Pound's *Cantos* are immersed
In quotations or concealed
Or erroneous references. I
Remember watching him work
In Rapallo when he was too
Excited to check his sources.
He was content to paraphrase
Or to insert in his line
A suggestive, brief phrase.
With Bill it was different.
He wanted specificity and
Accuracy in the quotations.
The early pages of *Paterson*
Are loaded with passages from
Old newspapers and histories
Of the region. And these are
Verbatim, not the poet's
Reconstruction of the events
As Pound would have done it.
So it was up to Van Vechten
To find graceful treatments of
Such interpolations. These
Alternations of prose with
Verse were one of the, to many
Readers, startling innovations
Of the poem. It's true that
His early *Spring and All* mixed
Prose and verse but that was in
1923 in a book which almost no
One saw. For Bill prose and verse
Were the same thing, as he
Expounded to Parker Tyler in
The letter of 1948, at left:

A novelty in the prose-poetry
Structure of *Paterson* was the
Inclusion of a number of verbatim
Letters Bill had received from
Friends. At first these seem
Irrelevant, but many, on second
Reading, appear to be subtly
Related to the work. They are
Peripheral elements in the
Grand mosaic of the poem, and
They are essential. In *I Wanted to
Write a Poem* of 1958 Bill had
Said: "I used documentary
Prose to break up the poetry,
To help shape the form of the
Poem. The poetic and the anti-
Poetic are all one piece."
Letters were from such as Pound
And the poet Richard Eberhart;
The novelist Josephine Herbst
And an adoring Rutherford
Neighbor, Kitty Hoagland, who
Often helped Bill out when
There were book-length scripts
To be typed; "Dreadful Edward"
Dahlberg, the most disagreeable
Author New Directions ever
Published (but *Because I Was
Flesh*, his autobiography, is a
Masterpiece); Gil Sorrentino,
Now an eminent avant-garde
Novelist; the enigmatic poet
Marcia Nardi; Allen Ginsberg
Who had grown up in Paterson.
(Allen persists in denying my
Anecdote that he became Bill's
Friend by leaving his poems
In the Williams' milk bottles,
But some myths are too good,
Too mythic, to be suppressed.)

Spring and All

by

William Carlos Williams

Marcia Nardi, impoverished
And embittered to the point
Of paranoia, living alone in
A shack in the woods near
Woodstock, was not for Bill
A romantic attachment. She
Was the symbol of woman
Victimized in a male society.
Her long letters inserted in
Paterson (one is eight full
Pages) insisting on having
Bill recognize her work and
Urging him to help her
Get it published, these pages
Expand her to a major female
Character till she becomes
As it were the figurative
Heroine of the epic. In the
Text Bill signed her letters
"Cress," the reference being
To Chaucer's "Criseyda."
The letters had more interest
For him than Nardi's verse,
Giving a social dimension
That the poem had lacked.
He called them "some of the
Best writing by a woman (or
By anyone else) I have seen
In years," and in one of his
Replies he tells her:

As he so often did when he
Wanted to encourage a young
Poet, Bill prevailed on me to
Put a group of Nardi's poems
In our New Directions annual.
I dragged my feet a bit—I
Found her work squishy—but
He insisted. At left are a few
Lines of typical Nardi; they
Are inferior to her letters.
Yet her letters give *Paterson*
A female contrapuntal voice

Excerpt from a letter to Nardi

Your letters show you to have one of
the best minds I have ever encoun-
tered. I say nothing of its reach
which I have had no opportunity to
measure but its truth and strength.
Your words as I read them have a
vigor and cleanliness to them which
constitute for me real beauty. I sin-
cerely and deeply admire you.

From poems by Marcia Nardi

The mind and flesh embrace
        each other.
Words yearning like breasts
        within a brain of stone—
Thought's fine perceptions
        thickening to press
A cageless mirrored body
        to her own.

In the midst of so much that is
Masculine. Nardi's letters
Became structurally important
For Bill; when he finished
Book Two and imagined that was
The end of the poem, for his
Coda he chose not a passage of
Verse but the longest of Nardi's
Letters, one that summarized
Her position in their exchange:

From a Marcia Nardi letter

My attitude toward woman's
wretched position in society and my
ideas about all the changes necessary
there, were interesting to you,
weren't they, in so far as they made
for *literature*? And you saw in one of
my first letters to you that my
thoughts were to be taken seriously,
because that too could be turned by
you into literature, as something dis-
connected from life.

Over the years the sending of
Poems dwindled considerably
But Bill was able to get some
Small grants for Nardi and a
Book of her poems was brought
Out by Alan Swallow early in
1956. A study of her work by
Elizabeth O'Neil was recently
Published. She died in 1990.

As *Paterson* first took shape
In Bill's mind the name of his
Persona was simply "Dr. Paterson."
But as its scope was expanded
He became "Noah Faitoute Paterson";
"Noah" was for surviving the
Flood of words that had threatened
To drown him. "Faitoute" was in
Honor of Bill's friend David
Lyle, Rutherford's omnididact,
Who could do anything and was
As *polumetis* as Odysseus: the
Man of many skills and endless
Devisings. "Dr. Noah Faitout
Paterson:" he could do it all.

In the *Cantos* Pound is his own
Protagonist. He puts down in the
Poem everything that has touched
His life in any way: every culture,
Every human connection; everything

He has read, seen or heard. These
Are his "phalanx of particulars."
Williams's protagonist covers less
Ground. "Dr. Paterson," wandering
Through the city, for the most
Part limits his range to the
Local, the environs of Paterson,
The people of New Jersey. But in
A sense as deep as with Pound
Language is the underlying subject
Of *Paterson*, even the motif of the
Poem if you will. A significant
Phrase which Bill often used
Is "a search for the redeeming
Language." Early in *Paterson*,
Referring to those whose lives
Seem to show little promise
Of meaning, he writes:

"The language, the language
            fails them
They do not know the words
            or have not
The courage to use them ."

Is "the language" a higher power,
More fundamental to him than
The oft repeated "no ideas but in
Things," which he borrowed from
The "nihil in intellectu quod non
Prius in sensu" of Scholasticism?

Despite the great pressures on
Him of having two intensive
Careers, his medical practice
And the writing of one book after
Another, being friends with Bill
Was, on the whole, happy sailing,
Up at least till the calamity of
David McDowell's intrigue. Bill
Had his moods, of course, but
Basically he was even-tempered,

*

THE

COMPLETE

COLLECTED POEMS OF

WILLIAM CARLOS

WILLIAMS

1906-1938

*

New Directions: Norfolk, Connecticut

24

With a good sense of humor, and
Ready to overlook my mistakes
And shortcomings as a publisher.
The actual amount of time we were
Able to spend together was not
Great. When I was finishing up
At Harvard (I didn't get my
Diploma until the end of term
In 1939), the trip down to see
Him in Rutherford was long by
Car. No planes then. Later when
I was running both New Directions
And the ski resort in Utah my
Visits were more infrequent.
But there were exceptions such
As the summer when my Aunt made
Floss and Bill the loan of her
Mountaintop cottage in Norfolk,
Where we had good talks and
Walks in the forest. A rest was
What Floss and Bill wanted. I
Saw that they got it. I fetched
Their groceries from the village
While my Aunt kept the local
Literary folk at bay. Another
Good get-together was a trip
With Bill to Charlottesville
Where the University was the
Sponsor of a conference on
Douglasite Social Credit. Pound
In his letters was constantly
Badgering Bill about monetary
Reforms, how it wasn't right
For banks to "create money" by
The issuance of credit, a power
Which belonged only to Congress
As set forth in the Constitution.
Douglas's twin theories of the
National Dividend and the Just
Price appealed to Bill because
He knew from the doctoring in
Poor communities that much was

Amiss in the social-economic
Order. His poems are tinged
Often with deep social concern.
A strain of social archaeology
Runs through *Paterson*. Bill's
Prose book *In the American Grain*
Looks at our history from
Red Eric to Lincoln to show how
We became what we are today as
Americans. But Bill never got
On the bandwagon of proletarian
Writing. He didn't let leftist
Friends such as Louis Zukofsky
Or Fred Miller push him into
Communism. I never thought of
Him as "political." I saw him
As humanitarian and libertarian.
Perhaps his only "political"
Poem is the famous "To Elsie,"
Which begins: "The pure products
Of America go crazy..." At the
University of Virginia conference
His talk was a moving statement
On "Social Credit as Anti-Communism."
He landed some good punches on
The bankers, but how many took
Him seriously? Bankers are as
Sacred as Baptist preachers. In
Book IV, Part II of *Paterson* Bill
Gave a full page to a Social
Credit tract announcing that
"The Constitution says: *To borrow
Money on the credit of the United
States*. It does not say: To borrow
Money from Private bankers."

What was Bill really like? Have
I come anywhere near catching
Him as he was? Probably not. His
Nature was complicated, though
It did not seem so on a first
Meeting. Then he was all charm.

A spontaneous charm so that one
Didn't have the feeling of being
Intentionally charmed. Inner
Conflicts were at first hidden
Under the surface, attitudes
That ranged from the puritan to
The bohemian. His was not a
Disciplined disposition. His
Personality floated free, it
Was governed by changing moods.
Herbert Leibowitz has written
Of Bill's character that it was
Full of "volatile cross-purposes."
Bill was generous, a giver of
Himself, but there were times
When he could suddenly turn
Brusque or indifferent. It
Occurred to me once, seeing
This happen, that the idea
For a poem had come into his
Head and it was more important
To him to work it out than to
Carry on the conversation. Bill
Could drift off for a while
And then return as if he had
Finished the poem, which he
Would then jot down on one
Of his medical prescription
Slips (hundreds of these are
Preserved in the Yale library
Archive). Bill's mind was of
Many layers. Some of them he
Seemed to want to conceal. He
Could shift quickly from a
Comic mood that was almost
Manic to a look and tone that
Suggested the bitterness of
Depression. But such episodes
Were brief, though once in
1952, following one of the
Strokes that plagued his later

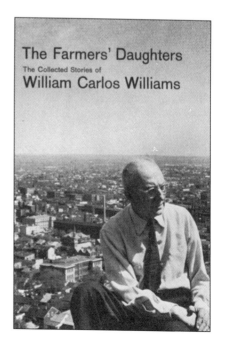

27

Years he felt it necessary to
Commit himself for treatment
In a sanitarium. His adviser
In such matters was the Boston
Poet-psychiatrist Merrill Moore,
The man who is said to have
Written fifty thousand sonnets.
Could there have been a genetic
Flaw that Bill inherited from
His mother, Elena Hoheb, partly
French from Martinique, partly
Dutch-Spanish-Jewish? No, that's
Far-fetched. Yet I remember her
As having a force of temperament
That went beyond eccentricity.
Bill was devoted to this tiny
Woman who had grown up in Puerto
Rico and Paris. When she came
To live at 9 Ridge Road and then
Became feeble he carried her up
And down stairs. He wrote a
Book about her, *Yes, Mrs. Williams*,
A reminiscence in which he put
Down her life as a girl and young
Woman in the islands and in Paris,
As she told it to him in a mixture
Of French, Spanish and English.
She died at the age of 102.

Of course the most understanding
Historian of Bill is his son
Dr. William Eric, who lives at
9 Ridge Road and had his office
There, a pediatrician like his
Father, until he recently retired.
*"Flossy, The Physical, Upbringing,
My Father the Doctor, Money, The
House, Food, Cars..."* these are
Some of the chapter titles for
The memoir that Bill Junior is
Writing about his dad. Here is
A scene that he remembers:

It was at night that Dad would call on apparently endless stores of energy, the tattoo of his typewriter providing a reassuring lullaby to which my brother Paul and I slept and awoke throughout childhood. I can recall the projection of his mood brought to me by the cadence of the keys—the smooth andante when all was happy and serene, and the interrupted staccato when the going got rough, the carriage slamming, and the paper ripped from the roller, balled, and heaved in the direction of the wastebasket. Night was his time to roar. Here was happiness, his love, Poetry...

And his description of his dad:

He was about five feet nine inches tall, shoe size 8D, hat size 7 1/4, shirt size 15 1/2-32, waist 32 to 34, with good posture in both standing and sitting positions. His weight fluctuated between 150 and 160 pounds and was well distributed.... His gait was purposeful. You felt he had a goal in mind as he strode along.... His hands were spadelike, a ditch-digger's, he used to say, with blunt tipped fingers and calloused palms. He was always clean shaven....The unruly jet black hair epitomized in his self portrait gradually gave way to baldness and an encircling halo of gray at the periphery of his skull. His eyes were dark brown, always searching, looking not only at you but into you, not impolitely but in an interested kind of way. There was nothing distinguished about his mouth. His dominating facial feature of course was his nose, which he recognized and early on glorified in his own poem 'Smell!'

> Oh strong-ridged and deeply hollowed
> nose of mine! what will you not be smelling?
> Must you taste everything? Must you know
>   everything?
> Must you have a part in everything?

He had a weathered skin of slightly olive hue. He and his father and brother Edgar walked hundreds of miles for the fun of it....He would take a trolley out of town 8 or 10 miles and then walk home. His sleep requirement was minimal....He needed physical work for an outlet, and there was about him an aura of tension, an invisible halo of potential that demanded a constant outlet. Yet he remained approachable. There was nothing obtrusive in his manner. People seemed to sense that here was a nice guy, who far from being offended, welcomed human contact.

The break, which happily was not
Permanent, between Bill and myself
Was not the fault or the intention
Of either one of us. It was the
Result of an intrigue engineered
By a meddlesome, self-serving rogue,
Now deceased, named David McDowell,
Whom I had hired in 1948 to help
Me run the sales and promotion side
Of New Directions. In his way Dave
Was brilliant as a sales manager;
If he had stuck to the job for which
He had been taken on all would have
Been well. The office crew liked him
And with his Southern charm, he
Was from Tennessee, he made a
Good impression for the firm
With reviewers and bookstore
People. His problem was that he
Was ambitious to the point of
Obsession. He wanted to get ahead,
He wanted power and money at
Any cost, morality be damned.
When David found that I was
Spending much time out in Utah
At the ski resort at Alta,
Which I was developing, he
Saw an opportunity to try to
Take control of New Directions.
Surreptitiously he began to
Cultivate certain ND authors,
Inviting them to lunch on the
Office expense account, but
Worse than this, he started to
Solicit manuscripts on his own
From other writers and from
Second-raters at that, people
Whose work I would never think
Of accepting. When I found out
I naturally gave him the bounce.
And from the nonchalant way he

Took it, I should have guessed
He had a larger plan in mind,
To wit, the alienation of Bill
From me and New Directions,
To whisk him away to another
Publisher. David soon rented
A house in Rutherford for his
Wife and himself, and he set
Out to pay court by making
Himself useful to Bill and
Subverting Bill's loyalty to
Me and New Directions. He told
Bill that our distribution was
Bad and that I was too tight to
Spend much money on advertising.
The latter is true; publishers
Know to their pain that highbrow
Literary books can't be sold by
Ads, only good reviews and word
Of mouth will sell them. As for
Distribution that depends on the
Enthusiasm of the salesmen. Ours
Loved our books and always did
A good job. Bill had never been
Concerned about these matters
Though he did chide me about my
Giving so much time to the ski
Lift business. He had reached a
Stage in his career when he
Wondered why he was not as famous
As Pound or Stevens. And he
Also worried about what Floss
Would live on after his death.
These anxieties made him fertile
Ground for McDowell's plotting.
That one, that Iago, made his
Next move by approaching the
President of Random House, that
Renowned editor of joke books,
Mr. Bennett Cerf, who readily
Took the bait, promising Iago

A job if he could come bearing
A three-book contract with Bill.
In short order Bill had become
A Random House author and, with
The help of his new editor,
Began assembling *Make Light of
It*, the collection of stories
That appeared in 1950. And so
Commenced the winter of my
Discontent that lasted eight
Years. The letters exchanged
Then, Bill's benign but adamant,
Mine awash with desperation and
Anguish, make painful reading
Now, but I guess they are part
Of literary history and should
At least be quoted from:

Bill to Jim, February 9, 1950:

I think I'll have a talk with McDowell now that he's with Random House
for I tell you frankly I'm not satisfied to let things run on the way
they've been going. It isn't that I've not been satisfied with our arrange-
ments in the past....It's the future I have to think of....So, if you'll agree,
I'd like to limit ourselves to this: that you bring out, now, the *Collected
Poems* as you have planned them and *Paterson IV* just as soon as I can
complete it, everything else to be crossed off the list. By this I shall gain
a free hand to try myself out, to see just how far I can go with sales.
...I'll never make any real cash through you. Nor have I wanted it until
now when either I must go on with Medicine or somehow or other get
me more income by writing, one or the other....

Jim to Bill, February 12, 1950:

Yours of the 9th to hand, and what a magnificent kick in the teeth that
is—administered, I may say, with a touch that is definitely deft, and
almost that one might think, of a practiced hand at this sort of thing;
which, of course, you aren't—the furthest thing from it—but how easily
we drift into it when the devil has planted the seed.
      Yes, a lovely reward for a decade of work and faith and sacrifice.
More power to you. I love the human race. The more they try to kick
me around the better I love them. Sure thing.

Frankly, Bill, I would never have dreamt that you, of all people, would fall this low. I suppose I have always carried you around on my special idealistic pedestal. You have always seemed to me the whitest of the white, the real human being—complete with sense and feeling.

Well, I am hurt. I am terribly hurt, I won't conceal it, and from the quarter I most trusted. A hundred times when other publishers have told me what faithless bastards writers are I have held you up as an example of loyalty. I feel exactly like Gretchen's brother in *Faust*. Look up the passage and read it for me.

But go your way—with my blessing. You are a loveable cuss, and I'll be sore for a few weeks, but it will pass. What you are doing is only human, and I've done plenty of things myself on a par with it. I can't complain.

Still in all, it's incredible, unbelievable. Have you no insight? Are you totally blind about your work and its nature? Do you really think that you can sell yourself to the masses, no matter how hard you try to write what they want?

All right...go to the big boys. They were swell to you about publishing *White Mule*, weren't they? They did a beautiful job on the *Collected Poems* didn't they? They fell over themselves didn't they to get a critic to write a book about you? They overwhelmed you, didn't they, with offers to keep the *American Grain* in print? Go to them. Rush. Run. Don't lose a second. Let them slobber their dirt all over your decency and your purity. And offer up to them as a little bribe *my* pride, and my life's devotion to an ideal. See how dirty they can make that too.

Well Bill, I'm sorry to have talked to you this way. It's not respectful, it's not friendly. But you have hurt me deeply and terribly, and the only way to get it out of my system is to talk right out, cauterize it, and then forget it.

You say you need money. Let me remind you that I offered to put you on a monthly check basis, as I do with [Henry] Miller, and you turned it down. I suppose you had your reasons.

Bill to Jim, March 9, 1950

I've made up my mind and having done so I write to you at once that you may know how we stand. I want you to do my poems as you have done in the past but my prose will go to someone else, probably Random House, under McDowell's editorship. This may prove somewhat of a wrench to both of us but there's no escaping it.

This chance has got to be taken if I'm to go on as a writer. For I can't make any money with you and I've got to try to earn at least a partial living by writing.

With this settled in my own mind I'm getting the new, two volume
Collected in order for your designer; it'll take me a few weeks to do it.
The short stories, before I give them to McDowell, I shall hold for two
weeks or until I can hear from you.

I hope this will satisfy you and that you will give the deal your
blessing but it is final.

What respect I might ever
Have had for David McDowell
Was blown away when his next
Fandango came to light a few
Weeks after he had moved
To Random House. This was
The story. One morning at
The New Directions office I
Wanted to check a point
In the manuscript of a book
We were publishing, a work
By a leading author. I kept
The manuscript in our safe.
But when I opened the safe
The manuscript was nowhere
To be found. I searched the
Shelves; it wasn't there.
Only two of us could work
That combination, I myself
And McDowell. What must have
Happened is obvious. He had
Taken his keys—his office
Keys and those to the building
—To a hardware store and had
Had them copied before he
Turned them in, then he had
Come up the fire stairs, which
Were open at night. Rare book
Dealers in the city would jump
At the chance to buy such a
Valuable manuscript and they
Wouldn't ask any questions
Either. Of course the police
Showed up. They investigated.
But nothing ever came of it:

They really had no evidence
Of a crime without an eye
Witness or recovery of the
Loot and they couldn't press
Charges. The thief was clear,
He had pulled off his revenge.
Where is the manuscript now?
In the hands of a private
Collector perhaps. In Texas?
England? Tokyo? Who knows?
Well, I had invoked Apollo,
God of the lyre, and also
Hermes, he who created the
Lyre from a tortoise shell,
To put a curse on McDowell.
They did. But they took their
Own sweet time about it. "Like
A green bay tree in springtime
The wicked shall flourish"—
So Cicero remarked somewhere.
(But I've forgotten the Latin.)
I made no effort to keep tabs
On McDowell. I just wanted to
Forget about him. I should have
Spotted him as a lemon and not
Hired him. Luckily I found a
Wonderful replacement before
Long in Bob MacGregor. Bob
Became the managing director
Of New Directions and ran it
Far better than I could have
For twenty years. He assumed
Complete charge in 1952 when I
Took leave to run Intercultural
Publications, a branch of the
Ford Foundation, which had me
Working most of my time abroad
In Europe and Asia. This was
An exciting change for me, I
Might be in Paris one day and
New Delhi the next, which kept
Me from dwelling on McDowell's

Rascality. He lasted only five
Years with Random House, where
He put out a Williams book each
Year, but Bill's books didn't
Sell much better with the big
Firm than they had with New
Directions. Predictably the
Romance with Cerf cooled off.
McDowell then found a friend,
A stockbroker, to back him in
His own company, but this was
A failure. He began to drink
Heavily and his nice little
Italian wife left him, taking
The children with her. After
That I heard of various short
Stints with other firms, but
Apparently the drink took over
And in time he went back to
Tennessee to an early death.

Life in the timeless East
Conduces to thought. In
Rangoon where with the help
Of U Thant who was running
Burma for his mystical friend
U Nu, I was assembling a
Perspectives of Burma, I had
Some instruction in meditation
From a wonderful lady named
Daw Khin Myo Chit. It was far
From instantaneous but I came
To see that the break with
Bill was pretty much my fault.
It had been wrong for me to
Spend so much time building
Ski lifts when my important
Work in life was to promote
The books of great poets. I
Determined somehow to make a
Mea culpa when I got back to
The States for good. Bill made

IMAGINATIONS
William Carlos Williams

Kora in Hell / Spring and All / The Descent of Winter
The Great American Novel / A Novelette & Other Prose

This easy for me by his own
Admission. He wrote me that
He realized that McDowell had
Used him and that he never
Wanted to see the man again.
He sent me the manuscript of
Book V of *Paterson,* declaring
His hope that we would be
Working together for the rest
Of his life. And so it was:
The Farmers' Daughters (the
Collected Stories) in 1961,
Many Loves (the Collected
Plays) in the same year, and
The last book of poems,
Pictures from Brueghel, which
Won a posthumous Pulitzer
Prize. Someone had given Bill
An album of Peter Brueghel
Paintings which he studied
Lovingly when his eyes were
Too tired to read print. These
Small descriptive poems are
Among his finest, glimpses
Into a past which he made
Contemporary in his vision.

Bill had taken me back, but
I still wanted to make my
Mea culpa to him. It must
Be formal, be in writing. It
Came to me that it should be
Done fictionally, and so
We have my story "A Visit,"
Which I published first in the
*William Carlos Williams News-
Letter* and then reprinted it
In my book *Random Stories.*

A young publisher, Marshall
MacDonald, drives out from
The city to make his apology

Something to Say

William Carlos Williams on Younger Poets

EDITED BY JAMES E. B. BRESLIN

To an elderly lawyer, Homer
Evans, who has suffered a
Stroke and had difficulty in
Finding his words. Driving
To Rutherford, MacDonald
Remembers many things about
Evans, but once there he is
So absorbed in his friend's
Conversation that he forgets
His mission and must return to
Complete it. Now as I reread
This story I find passages so
Right about Bill that I want
To quote them, even at the
Risk of repeating myself:
(The "he" is MacDonald, i.e.
JL. "Evans" of course is Bill.
The scene is at 9 Ridge Road.)

As he moved about the living room, taking it in, he heard a noise
from upstairs that he couldn't at first identify. It was a series of regular,
repeated sounds—first a kind of soft scrape and then a little thump...then
another scrape and thump. Suddenly it struck him; Evans must be drag-
ging himself downstairs, holding onto the bannister and dragging one leg
that had lost its mobility. It had gotten to that, the poor man could hard-
ly walk.

Evans looked older and his hair, what there was of it, was white,
but his figure was erect and his face ruddy and little lined for a man in
his late seventies. He was wearing spectacles with much thicker lenses—
the last bout in the hospital had been an operation for cataracts—but the
magnifying effect of the glasses made his eyes appear even more lively
than usual.

Evans had wonderful eyes. People remembered his eyes. He had
always been rather handsome in a crisp, lean-faced, eager-looking way,
but his eyes—brown with a dancing light in them, a merriment in
them—were the dominant feature. He could never have been much of a
poker player with such expressive eyes. Every movement from a mind
that was constantly in motion came through them. And now the magnifi-
cation of the lenses brought this play of feeling even closer to the person
near him.

In his poetry and in the essays—those 'prose pieces' with which he
had peppered the magazines for years, having his say in free-wheeling

style about anything that caught his eye or crossed his mind, from the new book by a young unknown to the probable effect of syphilis on Beethoven's music, Evans had always been as unrestrained in language, as unconcerned with taboos, as the newest would-be Rimbaud in the Village or North Beach. He had kept young with the youngest, and this had been a part of his appeal to successive generations. He didn't date. In his writing there was neither pontification nor withdrawal to a protected height. At seventy-five he could still be playful, at times a little ingenuous. With Evans creation was a matter of spontaneous (and sometimes almost continuous) combustion. Even on weekends he seldom had time to sit down to write with an open space of a whole morning before him. He had to catch the sparks as they flew. And how they flew! It was as if he were under a rain of cosmic rays, invisible pellets that showered him from God knew where, leaving marks on the sensitive plate in his mind which were immediately translated into images made of words. And the greater the pressure of law work, the more intense the bombardment. On vacations, when he did have free time, he wrote less than during the crowded rest of the year.

This way of writing had certainly influenced his style. With ellipses and leaps from image to image it was almost a poetic shorthand. There was something skeletal about his poems, even the long ones. Evans had no time to hammer out ornamentation, or to fashion much flesh between the bones. Part of the power of his poetry was in its very rawness, the fresh bite of the perception coming through to the reader as directly as it had to the poet in the simple, uncluttered phrasing. Of course, there was an elegance too; a man with an ear doesn't work with words fifty years for nothing. And it was not automatic writing; Evans did revise and rework. In the evenings, or on weekends, he would tinker with the sheets of drafts, trying different sequences and combinations. But he had never won the good opinion of the professor-critics for whom a poet must be as intricate as a complicated machine. Evans' work was not a happy hunting ground for the exegetes. An Evans poem said what it had to say at first reading. It offered no temptation to the academic maggots.

The force of life that had put together two such different impulses—the down-to-earth contact with the bodies of his clients and the wild escape into free imagination, into a kind of intentional dis-ordering, of poetry—came across to MacDonald as he sat close to Evans, more or less silently studying him as the old man searched for and found his words. A frail but electric man who all his life had had command of words, could summon them instantly to his use, and now, like the nightmare of a runner who cannot move his legs in his bad dream, a very nasty joke of fate, had to fight to bring them from his brain to his tongue. MacDonald could see how this injustice hurt Evans' pride. The poet became silent and began to look at his hands, rubbing one with the other. The hands were the only part of him which really betrayed his age. They were mottled with dark spots of brown and some of the veins stood up like blue vines on the skin.

"But these kids, these new young poets, they know what they've got to do and they're going on with it. I don't want them to copy me you understand. I give them hell when they're just doing what I did. They've got to go further with it. I don't know if I ever really made it a metric. But what is metric anyway? I read all the books about it once and I still don't know. But I know you've got to have it, it has to be there. It has to be speech and something else, too. It's nothing to do with scansion or tum-tee-tum but there has to be a base under the way the lines fall. I thought I had it the way I wanted it in 'Long Night,' I thought that was as far as I could go with it, but I'm not sure. I've still got more to do...and how am I going to do it now?

"But, I keep after it. I'm still pretty good with my left." Evans held up his hands in front of him and looked at them, as if they belonged to somebody else. "This one is pretty well shot—the fingers won't do what I want them to anymore. But I can still type with my left. I peck it out—without the capitals, it's too slow to hunt for that shift—and then Floss fixes it up for me. It still wants to come out. You'd think it would quit when everything else is going but it's still there. Some mornings it even wakes me up. I can't wait to get dressed or eat my breakfast. But it takes so long now to work it out. It's there and I know the words I want for it but I don't have them. I just have to sit till they come out of that fog in there. Floss can't help me on that. Sometimes it takes the whole morning to work it out, just ten or twenty lines in a whole morning—or I have to go back to it the next day.

"It's a funny thing that I can't quit. I sit here and take it...and you know I've never been able to write about death. I never had anything to say about it. All those poems and almost nothing about death in any of them. I don't like it, I'm afraid of it. I have to rest a lot now but I don't sleep much. I just have to lie there and face up to it—that pretty soon now I'm not going to be around. That's just a lot of shit about people being ready to die. And you know I've never been able to get anywhere with the idea of anything coming after. You go out like a light and you're out. I believe that. I don't expect anything else. But this thing won't stop. It's as strong now as it ever was, maybe stronger. And I don't think it's just habit. Maybe it is, but I don't think so. It's like there was somebody else in there. Look at me. I can hardly talk, this is more than I've talked in six months. I'm ready to fall apart, but this thing is at me just as hard as ever."

Halfway back to Manhattan
MacDonald becomes aware that
He has forgotten to tell Evans
About his remorse, which was
His purpose for the visit. He
Returns to 9 Ridge Road but
Finds Evans upstairs sleeping.
Fearful, he tells Floss he
Must see the old man anyway.

Evans raised himself on his pillows and snapped on the bedside table lamp. He was in his shirtsleeves with his tie off. He fumbled for his glasses on the table. MacDonald put them in his hand and sat down on the bed beside him. His words came tumbling out.

"I'm sorry to disturb you, but I forgot to tell you the most important thing, what I really came to see you for. You see I...I don't know just how to...well I have to make sure that you knew that I was sorry."

"Sorry? I don't see what..."

"About what happened between us. Only really it was what I did to you. I can understand that now and I wanted to tell you I was sorry I wrote those letters...and all the rest of it."

Evans was startled but then he understood and began to laugh. It wasn't a big laugh, but a little soft prolonged chuckle, and his head nodded from side to side as he pulled his good left hand out from beneath the blanket, felt for MacDonald's hand and covered it with his.

"Why, Marsh," he said, "you didn't have to come back here to tell me that. I knew that. I knew it when it happened. I knew you didn't mean all that stuff you wrote me."

"I guess I did mean it then. But I shouldn't have. And I don't now." He gave Evans' hand a squeeze and got up. "I'll get out of here now. I'm sorry I woke you up."

"You didn't," said Evans, "I was just lying here...thinking of...of...Venice, of all things." And as MacDonald left him, "But I'm glad you came back."

What I remember most about
Bill's illnesses, which began
With a heart attack in 1948,
Was his dogged determination
In fighting his way back from
Them. He wouldn't give in. At
A certain point he had to
Cut back on his doctoring
And then give it up entirely,
But nothing could stop him
From writing, even when he
Had to type with only one
Finger and mis-hit many keys
Anyway. After one of
His strokes he could hardly
Speak for several months.
Memory for words was very
Poor, but he never asked me
Not to come out to see him
At 9 Ridge Road (he refused
To go into the hospital).

Having visitors was part of
His battle for recovery.
For me these visits were
Agonizing. I wanted to help him
With the word I knew he was
Struggling to remember, but
He wouldn't let me. He would
Fight with his memory till
The right word finally came
Into his head. What guts he
Had and how much strength,
Considering what he'd been
Through to keep up the
Fight when anyone else in
His condition would have
Given up. Floss read aloud
To him and helped him with
His mail. The sons, Bill Jr.
And Paul, stopped by as often
As they could to spell her.
After a severe stroke, when

He was in bed in the home of
Charles Abbott, the curator
Of poetry at the University
Of Buffalo (where many of his
Papers are now housed) I did
My bit fixing up the plays
That he hadn't completed for
The *Many Loves* collection.
Composing the directions for
Staging to go into the book
Was simply beyond his grasp;
I wrote all of them for *The
Cure*, which is not a good
Play. It is a metaphor of
His own desperate situation,
Being the story of a young
Poet who is knocked out of
His senses in a motorcycle
Accident and restored to
Life by the girl who nurses
Him. It can also be seen as
A trope of the restoration
Of creativity through love.

During the period of his
Strokes Bill very belatedly
Achieved fame, at least in
The academic world and among
Serious readers of poetry.
He was no longer the obscure
Pediatrician in Rutherford
Who wrote a nutty poem about
A red wheelbarrow and some
Chickens. Almost overnight
Bill emerged as a major poet,
Ranked with Pound and Stevens.
There were honorary degrees
And more invitations to do
Readings than he was well
Enough to fulfill. There
Were prizes and conferences.
The only set-back came when

His appointment as Consultant
In Poetry at the Library of
Congress was cancelled.

To me one of the remarkable
Things about Bill's old age
Was his vision of what he
Called the "variable foot"
And his struggle to find it.
It was almost like an intense
Religious conversion, like
The pursuit of a metrical
Holy Grail. The exponent of
Free forms developed a need
For a traditional metric. I
Think it was a psychic need,
A throwback to his childhood
When his English-born
Father, William George, would
Read aloud (those were the days
Before radio and TV) almost all
Of Shakespeare, much Kipling
And endless verse from Palgrave's
Golden Treasury. When Bill began
To write his first substantial
Effort was an *Endymion* and next
In the 1909 pamphlet *Poems* it
Was wretched imitations of Keats,
Rhymed octosyllabic mush. (At
The end of his life Bill had me
Promise that none of this early
Trash would ever be reprinted.)
What extracted Bill from this
Drivel? Probably a combination
Of influences: reading Whitman,
Pound's sarcastic derision,
What he saw his contemporaries
Writing, Maxwell Bodenheim,
Mina Loy, the *Others* group
Led by Alfred Kreymborg, and
The poets in Harriet Monroe's
Poetry in Chicago. The work of

From *Poems of 1909*

Innocence can never perish;
Blooms as fair in looks that cherish
Dim remembrance of the days
When life was young, as in the gaze
Of youth himself all rose-yclad,
Whom but to see is to be glad.

Avant-garde French painters
In the Armory Show of 1913, who
Were abandoning representation
In favor of abstraction, was
Important too. Soon Bill gave
Up rhyme and the tum-tee-tum
Meters. Within ten years he
Had perfected his own New
Jersey brand of vers libre,
As in "The Revelation" (1915):
He went on to become the best
Line-breaker of his time; i.e.
He had the most sensitive ear
For judging which word should
End a line and how the syntax
Should turn against the flow
Of lines, which is the skill
That shapes free verse and gives
It organic form. After that came
The more visual patterning of
The text in *Paterson*, lines
Irregularly spaced and floating
On the field of the page. Then
The next innovation, I think in
About 1953, was the "triadic
Line," which was a step-down
Line of medium length divided
Into three roughly equal parts,
Beginning at the left margin
And cascading gently down to
The right over a series of
Evenly spaced indentations. It
Is the stanzaic base for
Asphodel, That Greeny Flower,
Bill's 30-page tribute and
Apology to Floss. Like this:

From "The Revelation"

I awoke happy, the house
Was strange, voices
Were across a gap
Through which a girl
Came and paused,
Reaching out to me—

Then I remembered
What I had dreamed—
A girl
One whom I knew well
Leaned on the door of my car
And stroked my hand—

I shall pass her on the street
We shall say trivial things
To each other
But I shall never cease
To search her eyes
For that quiet look—

Of asphodel, that greeny flower,
    like a buttercup
        upon its branching stem—

save that it's green and wooden—
    I come, my sweet
        to sing to you.

We lived long together
    a life filled,
        if you will,

with flowers ...

The "triadic line" appealed to
Bill for two reasons. It gave
Him more opportunities to use
His gift for beautiful line
Breaks. Second was a practical
Advantage: when he was obliged
To give up his work at the
Hospital because of the strokes
The other doctors made him a
Present of a modern typewriter
That had many improved features.
One of them was a carriage-back
Stop system; he could set the
Stops for the three indents of
The "triadic line" and save the
Bother of trying to get the
Alignment with his shaky hand.

So we come to the final hoped
For invention of the "variable
Foot," a term first used by Poe.
"Bill was convinced," writes
Herbert Leibowitz, "that our
Poetry needed to find a new
Measure for contemporary
Realities." Bill dreamed that
If he could find the key to
This new measure and master it,
It could become his metrical

Signature. More than that,
And here I'm theorizing, he
Didn't tell me so directly,
It would give him the authority
Of using a disciplined line,
One that could be scanned,
Yet would be free for variety,
For substitutions in the feet.
"He didn't want a rigid foot,"
Leibowitz goes on, "he wanted
A stable foot." The "variable
Foot" would be confirmation that
His poetry could take its place
In the stream of the English
Verse tradition, especially
The great Renaissance poetry
Such as Campion's beautiful:

Harke, al you ladies that do sleep:
        the fayry queen Proserpina
Bids you awake and pitie them that weep:
        you may doe in the darke
What the day doth forbid:
        feare not the dogs that barke,
                Night will have all hid.

Of course Bill was not urging
Rhyme, it was the breaks in the
Scansion that interested him,
And probably also the fact that
Campion too was a doctor.
American speech rhythms were to
Be regularized in some way.
It was a formidable task, but
Much on Bill's mind, as some
Letters to his friends, the
Poet Richard Eberhart and the
Professor John Thirlwall, show:

WCW to Eberhart - 10/23/53:

> What Pound did not realize, nor Yeats either, is that a new order had
> dawned in the makeup of the poem. The measure, the actual measure, of
> the lines is no longer what Yeats was familiar with. Or Pound either,
> except instinctively.
>
> Whitman with his so-called free verse was wrong: there can be no
> absolute freedom in verse. You must have a measure but a relatively
> expanded measure to exclude what has to be excluded and to include
> what has to be included. It is a technical point but a point of vast impor-
> tance.

WCW to Eberhart - 5/23/54:

> I have never been one to write by rule, even by my own rules. Let's
> begin with the rule of counted syllables, in which all poems have been
> written hitherto. That has become tiresome to my ear.
>
> Finally, the stated syllables, as in the best of present-day free verse,
> have become entirely divorced from the beat, that is the measure. The
> musical pace proceeds without them.
>
> By measure I mean musical pace. Now, with music in our ears the
> words need only be taught to keep as distinguished an order, as chosen a
> character, as regular, according to the music, as in the best of prose.
>
> By its *music* shall the best of modern verse be known and the
> *resources* of the music. The refinement of the poem, its subtlety, is not to
> be known by the elevation of the words but—the words don't so much
> matter—by the resources of the *music*.

That sentence about sound
Mattering more than sense
Would be astonishing given
The nature of his work if we
Were meant to take it literally.
I suspect Bill was only
Inveighing against excessive
Rhetoric and decoration.

WCW to Thirlwall - 1/13/55:

> If the measure by which the poem is to be recognized has at present
> been lost, it is only lost in the confusion which at present surrounds our

lives. We don't, any more, know how to measure the lines and therefore have convinced ourselves that they can't be measured.

You cannot break through old customs, in verse or social organization, without drastically changing the whole concept and also the structure of our lives all along the line.

That is merely and magnificently the birth of a new measure supplanting the old—something we hardly hoped to dare.

In the eight years between this
Letter and Bill's death in 1963
One can find a good many more
References to the "variable foot,"
Including the lines in *Asphodel,*
That Greeny Flower:

"...and set dancing
                to a measure,

a new measure!
        Soon lost.
                The measure itself

has been lost
        and we suffer for it.
                We come to our deaths

in silence. ..."

But where is the passage I've
Always hoped to find, no scholar
Has ever pointed me to it, where
Bill demonstrates that he has
Found his grail, the passage
Where he declares without any
Equivocation: "this is my
Variable foot," then defines
Its properties precisely and
Puts the scansion marks to it.

Is there a clue in a poem in
His last book, *Pictures from
Brueghel,* a poem in nine parts,
Which is provocatively titled

"Some Simple Measures in the
American Idiom and the Variable
Foot"? Here, at right, are the
First and last parts. What
Beat do you hear in them?
Can these lines be scanned in
Any formal way? Or can one find
Any significant variations from
What Bill was writing in 1921,
Say at the time of *Sour Grapes.*
The lines are short, the diction
Is skeletal, the typographical
And syllabic patterns are quite
Regular and in large part visual.
I'm afraid for me the poems
Don't show any new measure or
A different rhythm. Am I wrong?

Why didn't Bill find the
"Variable foot" when he was
So eager to have it? Was it
Just a mirage? Or was it
Because other poets and
Critics never took his search
Seriously and supported him in
It? Which is not to say that
In his later years Bill was
Neglected by the academics
As he had been when he was a
Young poet. But the "variable
Foot," given the problems he
Had in showing a scansion for
It, presented difficulties
Even for readers who had long
Admired his work. This failure
Of ready comprehension both
Worried and wounded him. So
He was cheered when an old
Friend, Professor Mary Ellen
Solt of Indiana University,
Who had written about his
Poetry in the literary

I. Exercise in Timing

Oh
the sumac died
it's
the first time
I
noticed it

IX. The Stolen Peonies

What I got out of women
was difficult
to assess Flossie

not you
you lived with me
many years you remember

that year
we had the magnificent
stand of peonies

how happy we were
with them
but one night

they were stolen
we shared the
loss together thinking

of nothing else for
a whole day
nothing could have

brought us closer
we had been
married ten years

Journals for many years,
Invited him to Indiana and
Set up a reading for him to
Which many members of the
English Department came.
Solt's analysis of the
"Variable Foot" led to a
Discussion which helped Bill
Clarify his theory and gave
The encouragement and self-
Confidence he needed to go
On with his experiment.

Bill's last year was an
Oppressive sadness for me,
Though his courage was an
Inspiration, his refusal to
Give up on his writing, his
Determination to learn how to
Type again, his handwriting
Being so shaky that even Floss
Could hardly decipher it. What
Could I do to help or comfort
Him? He didn't want a nurse
Hanging around the house. I
Tried to stop by 9 Ridge Road
Now and then. For a few minutes
He would listen to my gossip
About writers, and even smile,
But then he would tire and
Send me away. I felt pretty
Certain from watching him
That ideas for poems were
Forming in his mind even if
He couldn't put them down. Did
I detect occasionally some of
The old snap in his eyes?
I no longer recall the exact
Dates of his strokes, but I
Saw gradual deterioration
Of the whole physical plant.
His eyes were weaker, he took

Longer to summon the words he
Wanted, his reactions were
Slower. Floss said he was
Losing his appetite, some
Evenings all he would eat was
Porridge or a poached egg. He
Was allowed a shotglass of
Bourbon after his dinner but
It didn't perk him up for
Long. He worried about when
Pictures from Brueghel, the
Last book of poems, would be
Ready. Why were the printers
So slow? I took to bringing
The galleys out to him in
Installments as they were
Ready. I read them to him
Line by line, very slowly,
Re-reading when he signaled
Me to pause. When he wanted
A correction I'd sit beside
Him on the sofa and painfully
We'd work it out together.
His sense for words, of which
Words would sound well together,
Was as sharp as ever. But he
Became tired so quickly.

One day when I arrived at
9 Ridge Road in the late
Morning I saw an unexpected
And encouraging sight. Bill
Had had a burst of energy and
Was typing, with one finger,
At the dining room table. Floss
Put her head in from the kitchen
To tell me, "Don't disturb him,
He's practicing by trying to
Write me a letter." The floor
Was littered with balls of
Paper Bill had crumpled up
And thrown away. When he was

Tired and stopped his work I
Picked up one of the balls
And deciphered it later
Out in the car. The typing
Was mostly wrong, but this
Is what he wanted to say.

Dear Floss thank you for everything
forgive me   I always loved you Bill

Miraculously, as Bill kept up
His practice on the machine
He made much improvement so
That his letters were easier to
Understand and Floss could mail
Them. Here is the last letter
To me that he typed himself.

Dear Jim

I fnally got your letter enclosing your letter enclocussing your
letter which was so ompportant foe me, thannkuok youn very
much. In time this fainful bsiness will will soonfeul will soon be
onert. Tnany anany goodness. IfSlossieeeii wyyonor wy sinfsigna-
ture.
    I hope I hope I make it   Bill

Bill's battle, the physical battle,
Was ended on March 4, 1963. He had
Died in his sleep in the night;
Floss found him peacefully silent
When she went to wake him for
Breakfast. Not long after, *Pictures
From Brueghel* was awarded the prize
He had never had when he was alive,
The Pulitzer. From then on there
Was steady growth in the popular
Acceptance of Bill's work and its
Recognition in academic circles,
Where it is widely taught in the
Curriculum. He is in all the big

54

Anthologies. His books have been
Translated into many languages.
The poet who had to pay to get
His first five books published
Is now enshrined as one of the
Great American literary figures.

Bill's funeral was unusual because
The young minister, almost with
Rage, excoriated the prosperous
Elements of Rutherford for never
Realizing that they had a
Genius among them; few of the
"Best people" of the town had
Used "the poet" for their doctor.
As we know from his short stories
His practice was among the poor
And the working people, some of
Whom could only pay him with a
Sack of vegetables from their
Gardens. But Bill had had his
Say about funerals in his poem
"Tract," written back in 1916:

Tract

I will teach you my townspeople
how to perform a funeral
for you have it over a troop
of artists—
unless one should scour the world—
you have the ground sense necessary.

See! the hearse leads.
I begin with a design for a hearse.
For Christ's sake not black—
nor white either—and not polished!
Let it be weathered—like a farm wagon—
with gilt wheels (this could be
applied fresh at small expense)
or no wheels at all:
a rough dray to drag over the ground.

Knock the glass out!
My God—glass, my townspeople!
For what purpose? Is it for the dead
to look out or for us to see
how well he is housed or to see
the flowers or the lack of them—
or what?
To keep the rain and snow from him?
He will have a heavier rain soon:
pebbles and dirt and what not.
Let there be no glass—
and no upholstery, phew!
and no little brass rollers
and small easy wheels on the bottom—
my townspeople what are you thinking of?

A rough plain hearse then
with gilt wheels and no top at all.
On this the coffin lies
by its own weight.

                         No wreaths please—
especially no hot house flowers.
Some common memento is better,
something he prized and is known by:
his old clothes—a few books perhaps—
God knows what! You realize
how we are about these things
my townspeople—
something will be found—anything
even flowers if he had come to that.
So much for the hearse.

For heaven's sake though see to the driver!
Take off the silk hat! In fact
that's no place at all for him—
up there unceremoniously
dragging our friend out to his own dignity!
Bring him down—bring him down!
Low and inconspicuous! I'd not have him ride
on the wagon at all—damn him—
the undertaker's understrapper!

Let him hold the reins
and walk at the side
and inconspicuously too!

Then briefly as to yourselves:
Walk behind—as they do in France,
seventh class, or if you ride
Hell take curtains! Go with some show
of inconvenience; sit openly—
to the weather as to grief.
Or do you think you can shut grief in?
What—from us? We who have perhaps
nothing to lose? Share with us
share with us—it will be money
in your pockets.
                    Go now
I think you are ready.

* * *

At the burial, which took
Place on a slope in the old
Rutherford Cemetery, occurred
An event which to most of those
Present was comical, like the
Clowns piling out of a car at
The circus, but to me, who knew
How to interpret it, was truly
Prophetic. After the service
A huge, unidentifiable, very
Ancient black sedan drew up
On the adjacent roadway, and
From it emerged not one, not
Five, but *ten* blackclad figures,
Dressed in what they thought
Suitable for a funeral, rented
Or borrowed, to join the other
Mourners. They were the leading
Young poets of New York come
To pay homage to the great old
Poet they so much admired. It
Was a striking moment. And it
Was, I knew, symbolic of the

Hundreds and thousands of young
Poets who in the future would
Honor Williams and acknowledge
His influence in their work,
And I one among them.

Now I have talked enough in
Telling what I had to tell.
As an afterpiece I will add
(A poem by Kenneth Rexroth
Called "A Letter to William
Carlos Williams," which speaks
For us all and is one of the
Most expressive poems ever
Written by one poet about
Another. Here I will only say
That after all the talk about
His particular achievements
In language, form, and topical
Attitudes Bill remains a person
As complex and indefinable as
Any, yet in his work (as he
Was in his life) believable,
Lovable, and knowable; a great
Poet among all the other great
Poets from first to last to
Whom we turn for consolation,
Friendship, pleasure, wisdom,
And warmth of human feeling.

A Letter to William Carlos Williams

Dear Bill,

When I search the past for you,
Sometimes I think you are like
St. Francis, whose flesh went out
Like a happy cloud from him,
And merged with every lover—
Donkeys, flowers, lepers, suns—
But I think you are more like
Brother Juniper, who suffered
All indignities and glories
Laughing like a gentle fool.
You're in the *Fioretti*
Somewhere, for you're a fool, Bill,
Like the Fool in Yeats, the term
Of all wisdom and beauty.
It's you, stands over against
Helen in all her wisdom,
Solomon in all his glory.

Remember years ago, when
I told you you were the first
Great Franciscan poet since
The Middle Ages? I disturbed
The even tenor of dinner.
Your wife thought I was crazy.
It's true, though. And you're 'pure,' too,
A real classic, though not loud
About it—a whole lot like
The girls of the Anthology.
Not like strident Sappho, who
For all her grandeur, must have
Had endometriosis,
But like Anyte, who says

Just enough, softly, for all
The thousands of years to remember.

It's a wonderful quiet
You have, a way of keeping
Still about the world, and its
Dirty rivers, and garbage cans,
Red wheelbarrows glazed with rain,
Cold plums stolen from the icebox,
And Queen Anne's lace, and day's eyes,
And leaf buds bursting over
Muddy roads, and splotched bellies
With babies in them, and Cortes
And Malinche on the bloody
Causeway, the death of the flower world.

Nowadays, when the press reels
With chatterboxes, you keep still,
Each year a sheaf of stillness,
Poems that have nothing to say,
Like the stillness of George Fox,
Sitting still under the cloud
Of all the world's temptation,
By the fire, in the kitchen,
In the Vale of Beavor. And
The archetype, the silence
Of Christ, when he paused a long
Time and then said, 'Thou sayest it.'

Now in a recent poem you say,
'I who am about to die.'
Maybe this is just a tag
From the classics, but it sends
A shudder over me. Where
Do you get that stuff, Williams?
Look at here. The day will come
When a young woman will walk
By the lucid Williams River,
Where it flows through an idyllic
News from Nowhere sort of landscape,
And she will say to her children,
'Isn't it beautiful? It

Is named after a man who
Walked here once when it was called
The Passaic, and was filthy
With the poisonous excrements
Of sick men and factories.
He was a great man. He knew
It was beautiful then, although
Nobody else did, back there
In the Dark Ages. And the
Beautiful river he saw
Still flows in his veins, as it
Does in ours, and flows in our eyes,
And flows in time, and makes us
Part of it, and part of him.
That, children, is what is called
A sacramental relationship.
And that is what a poet
Is, children, one who creates
Sacramental relationships
That last always.'

With love and admiration,

Kenneth Rexroth.

ACKNOWLEDGMENTS

Grateful acknowledgment is made to New Directions Publishing Corporation for permission to quote from the following copyrighted works of William Carlos Williams: *The Autobiography of William Carlos Williams* (Copyright 1948, 1951 by William Carlos Williams); *The Collected Poems of William Carlos Williams, Volume I, 1909-1939* (Copyright 1938 by New Directions Publishing Corporation); *The Collected Poems of William Carlos Williams, Volume II, 1939-1962* (Copyright © 1944, 1953, 1962 by William Carlos Williams); *I Wanted to Write a Poem* (Copyright © 1958 by William Carlos Williams); *Many Loves & Other Plays* (Copyright 1948 by William Carlos Williams); *Paterson* (Copyright © 1946, 1948, 1949, 1951, 1958 by William Carlos Williams); *The Selected Letters* (Copyright © 1957 by William Carlos Williams); *White Mule* (Copyright 1937 by New Directions Publishing Corporation).

Previously unpublished material by William Carlos Williams, Copyright © 1995 by William Eric Williams and Paul H. Williams; used by permission of New Directions Publishing Corporation, agents.

Quotations from *William Carlos Williams and James Laughlin: Selected Letters*, edited by Hugh Witemeyer, (Copyright © 1989 by James Laughlin; Copyright © 1989 by the Estate of William Carlos Williams) including sections from "A Visit" (Copyright © 1978 by James Laughlin) are used by permission of W. W. Norton & Co., Inc. and James Laughlin.

Quotations from *The Last Word: The Letters of Marcia Nardi and William Carlos Williams* (Copyright © 1994 by Elizabeth O'Neil) used by permission of the University of Iowa Press and Elizabeth O'Neil.

Kenneth Rexroth's "A Letter to William Carlos Williams" (Copyright 1949 by Kenneth Rexroth) is from *The Collected Shorter Poems of Kenneth Rexroth*; used by permission of New Directions Publishing Corp.

Sections from William Eric Williams's manuscript about his father are used with the kind permission of William Eric Williams.

Photo and picture credits: all Williams family photographs of William Carlos Williams or others (p. 5; p. 28 – Raquel Hélenè Rose Hoheb Williams; p. 42 – 9 Ridge Road, Rutherford, NJ; p. 43 – WCW and Florence H. Williams; p. 53) courtesy of William Eric Williams and Paul H. Williams; all book jackets courtesy of the New Directions archives; all non-family photographs of WCW are from New Directions files and are here identified by photographer (cover and frontispiece, Charles Sheeler; p. 27, Eve Arnold; p. 36, Irving Wellcome; p. 44, Tram; p. 47, James Laughlin; p. 63, John D. Schiff); drawing of WCW on p. 37 by Ben Shahn; photograph of James Laughlin on p. 8 taken in the New Directions office, 1939, by Polly Storey; photograph of James Laughlin on p. 62 from Laughlin family photographs; drawing of the falls over the Passaic River at Paterson, NJ, by Earl Horter, courtesy of the State Library of New Jersey.